LIFE IN A DOLPHIN POD

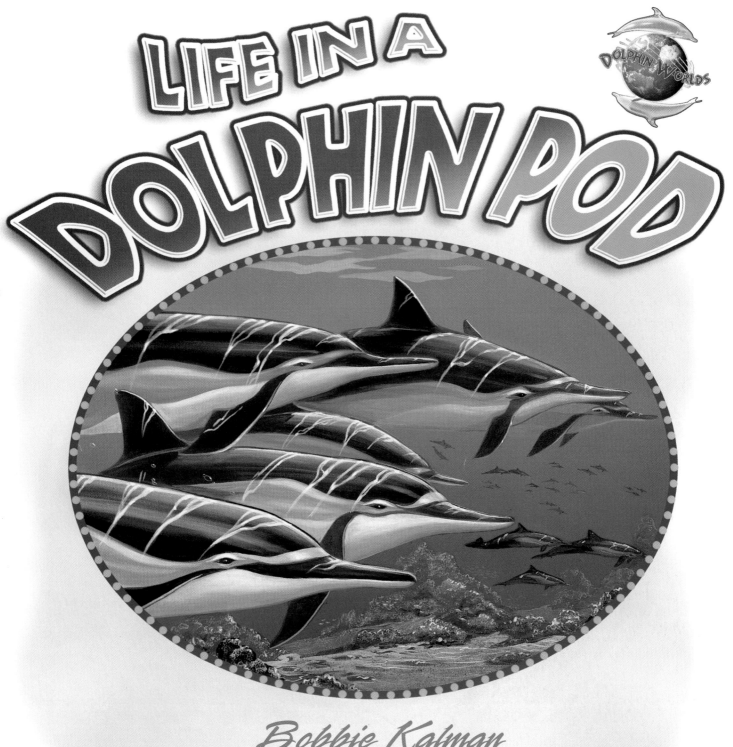

Bobbie Kalman

🌳 Crabtree Publishing Company

www.crabtreebooks.com

Created by Bobbie Kalman

For Roberta Goodman,
with much admiration for your work with dolphins

Author and Publisher
Bobbie Kalman

Editorial director
Niki Walker

Editors
Amanda Bishop
Rebecca Sjonger

Art director
Robert MacGregor

Design
Bobbie Kalman
Campbell Creative Services
Samantha Crabtree

Production coordinator
Heather Fitzpatrick

Photo research
Samantha Crabtree
Laura Hysert

Consultant
Patricia Loesche, Ph.D.,
Animal Behavior Program,
Department of Psychology,
University of Washington

Special thanks to
Diane Sweeney and Dolphin Quest, Lindsey Potter

Photographs
© Steve Bloom/stevebloom.com: cover
Photos courtesy of Dolphin Quest Hawaii, located at the Kahala Mandarin
    Oriental Hawaii: pages 7 (center), 22
Bobbie Kalman (taken at Dolphin Quest Hawaii at the Kahala Mandarin
    Oriental Hawaii): page 7 (top and bottom)
© Phillip Colla/oceanlight.com: pages 26, 27 (top)
© Michael S. Nolan/wildlifeimages.net: pages 10, 16 (top), 27 (bottom)
Tom Stack & Associates, Inc., : Jeff Foott: page 16 (bottom)
© James D. Watt/wattstock.com: pages 20, 21 (both)
Sea Pics/seapics.com: © Doug Perrine: pages 4, 13 (top), 14, 29;
    © Hiroto Kawaguchi: page 15 (bottom); © Masa Ushioda: page 5;
    © Ingrid Visser: page 31
© Brandon Cole/brandoncole.com: pages 11, 28
Other images by Digital Vision and Digital Stock

Illustrations and artwork
© Apollo/networldesign.com/apollo/: title page, pages 3, 17, 18-19,
Barbara Bedell: pages 14, 23 (bottom), 24-25, 27, 29, 31
© Jeff Wilkie/jeffwilkie.com: page 23 (top)
Tiffany Wybouw: all borders and decorative dolphins, pages 6, 8-9,
    23 (center)

Crabtree Publishing Company

www.crabtreebooks.com   1-800-387-7650

PMB 16A
350 Fifth Avenue
Suite 3308
New York, NY
10118

612 Welland Avenue
St. Catharines
Ontario
Canada
L2M 5V6

73 Lime Walk
Headington
Oxford
OX3 7AD
United Kingdom

Cataloging-in-Publication Data
Kalman, Bobbie
   Life in a dolphin pod / Bobbie Kalman.
      p. cm. -- (Dolphin worlds)
Includes index.
   ISBN 0-7787-1164-1 (RLB) -- ISBN 0-7787-1184-6 (pbk.)
   1. Dolphins--Behavior--Juvenile literature. 2. Social behavior in
animals--Juvenile literature. [1. Dolphins.] I. Title.
QL737.C432 K378 2003
599.53'15--dc21
                                                    LC 2002012081

Contents

Social animals

Dolphins are social animals that prefer to live in the company of other dolphins. Dolphins do not live with other dolphins for company alone, however. They do it to survive! Living as part of a group helps them find and catch food more easily. Group members also help protect one another from **predators** such as sharks and larger dolphins.

When studying the behavior of dolphins, it is important to remember that dolphins are intelligent animals with individual personalities. This book talks about how scientists have seen dolphin groups behave, but dolphins never stop surprising people!

Group sizes

Dolphin groups can contain as few as two or three dolphins or as many as thousands. **Oceanic dolphins**, or dolphins that live in open ocean waters, belong to large groups. In the open ocean, there is plenty of food, and members of dolphin groups often cooperate in finding and trapping **prey**. **Coastal dolphins**, or dolphins that live close to shorelines, hunt and travel in much smaller groups because there is less food and there are fewer predators near the coasts.

Group names

Many people use the word **pod** to refer to a group of dolphins, but scientists also use other names to describe dolphin groups.

A **herd** is a group of one **species**, or type, of dolphin whose members share a **home range**, or area of activity.

A **school** is a large group made up of several herds. It may contain more than one dolphin species.

A **subgroup** is a smaller group that does not always travel with the herd but comes back to it.

A **family pod** is a stable unit of mothers and their offspring that may contain sons and uncles.

A **nursery pod** is a group of mothers and calves.

There are many sharks in open ocean waters. When dolphin schools, such as this Hawaiian spinner school, swim in a tight group, there is less chance that a predator will capture a single one. In coastal waters, there are fewer predators, so dolphin groups do not need the protection of large schools.

A bit about dolphins

Dolphins are **vertebrates**, or animals with spinal columns. Their flexible spines allow them to move their tails up and down as they swim. Their rib cages protect organs such as the heart, lungs, and stomach. Their neck **vertebrae**, or bones, are fused (see diagram below), making dolphins more **streamlined**, or smoothly shaped.

Dolphins are mammals

Dolphins are not fish. They are **marine mammals**, or mammals that live in the sea. Even though dolphin ancestors walked on land, dolphins cannot live out of water.

As mammals, dolphins are **warm-blooded**. Dolphin mothers give birth to live babies that **nurse**, or feed, on their mothers' milk.

Dolphins are cetaceans

Dolphins belong to a group of marine mammals called **cetaceans**. Cetaceans are divided into two smaller groups: **baleen whales** and **toothed whales**. Baleen whales have huge curtains of baleen in their mouths for trapping food. Toothed whales, which include sperm whales, belugas, porpoises, and dolphins, have as many as 250 cone-shaped teeth.

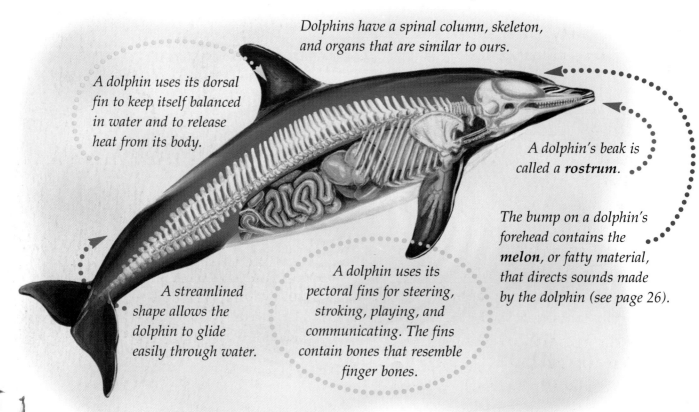

Dolphins have a spinal column, skeleton, and organs that are similar to ours.

A dolphin uses its dorsal fin to keep itself balanced in water and to release heat from its body.

*A dolphin's beak is called a **rostrum**.*

*The bump on a dolphin's forehead contains the **melon**, or fatty material, that directs sounds made by the dolphin (see page 26).*

A streamlined shape allows the dolphin to glide easily through water.

A dolphin uses its pectoral fins for steering, stroking, playing, and communicating. The fins contain bones that resemble finger bones.

How a dolphin breathes

A dolphin breathes through a single blowhole that is connected to its lungs but not to its mouth or stomach. It can swim, breathe, and eat all at the same time and not choke on its food. A strong muscle opens and closes the blowhole. To learn more about how a dolphin breathes, see page 18.

Dolphins are predators

Most dolphins eat fish and squid, but some larger dolphins prey on marine mammals. A few species even eat other dolphins! Dolphins catch their food with their teeth, but they do not chew it. They swallow their food whole or tear it into large chunks. Dolphins get all the water they need from the food they eat, so they never have to take a drink.

Hiding and keeping warm

Two-toned coloring provides a dolphin with **camouflage**. When seen from below, a dolphin's light-colored belly blends in with the sunlit ocean surface. When seen from above, its gray back is hard to make out against the dark, deep ocean waters. This pattern of light and dark is called **countershading**. Dolphins have a layer of **blubber**, or fat, under their skin. Blubber keeps in body heat and insulates dolphins from cold ocean water.

A dolphin takes in air and blows it out through its blowhole.

Dolphins swallow fish whole. Down the hatch!

A dolphin's belly is light, and its back is dark.

Many kinds of dolphins

There are about 34 to 36 species of "true" dolphins, or dolphins that belong to the family Delphinidae. River dolphins and porpoises do not belong to this family, but **blackfish** do. Blackfish are not fish—they are dolphins that are called "whales." There are six species of blackfish: orcas or killer whales, false killer whales, long- and short-finned pilot whales, pygmy killer whales, and melon-headed whales. They are shown on this page. Many of the other Delphinidae species are also shown on these pages.

orca
(killer whale)

pygmy
killer whale

short-
finned pilot
whale

long-finned pilot
whale

false killer whale

bottlenose dolphin

melon-headed
whale

Risso's dolphin

southern right whale dolphin

northern right whale dolphin

Indo-Pacific humpback
dolphin

Irrawaddy dolphin

rough-toothed dolphin

Fraser's dolphin

Atlantic humpback dolphin

pantropical spotted dolphin

striped dolphin

Atlantic white-sided dolphin

Pacific white-sided dolphin

long-beaked common dolphin

Atlantic spotted dolphin

spinner dolphin

short-beaked common dolphin

dusky dolphin

Peale's dolphin

Clymene dolphin

Heaviside's dolphin

hourglass dolphin

tucuxi

Hector's dolphin

Commerson's dolphin

black dolphin (Chilean dolphin)

white-beaked dolphin

9

Large dolphin schools

Dolphins group themselves in ways that help them survive. Some dolphins form large schools of hundreds or thousands of dolphins. Many of these dolphins live in deep ocean waters, but some also live near shorelines. Large dolphin schools often break up into smaller groups for part of a day or a season.

Spinner dolphins

Spinner dolphins are named after the way they spin as they leap out of water. No one knows why they spin. Spinners live in **fission-fusion**, or splitting-joining, societies. Hundreds of spinners come together at night to hunt and feed on the fish, shrimp, and squid that live in deep ocean waters. To find prey, they spread out in groups that may cover miles of the ocean. They then assemble quickly to trap the fish they have found. After hunting all night, small subgroups of spinners enter shallow bays to rest in rows alongside one another. In the afternoons, spinners gather again to play.

Changing subgroups

Spinners constantly change their subgroup members. There seem to be no rules about who spends time with whom, but adult males and females are the core of each subgroup. They join up with **juveniles** and mom-and-calf pairs. Adult males often act as scouts and swim ahead to alert the herd about predators or prey. Nursery pods consist of mothers, calves, and adult females that babysit calves during a hunt. When a school is large or rowdy, nursery pods swim on its fringes to protect the calves from injury. Older dolphins sometimes stay on the fringes as well, away from the more energetic spinners.

Dusky populations

Dusky dolphins live in the coastal waters off South America, South Africa, and New Zealand. The behavior of the different populations is determined by the location and behavior of the prey they hunt.

Day-to-dusk duskies

South American duskies feed mostly during the day but have been seen feeding at dusk as well. They hunt for schools of anchovies in subgroups of eight to ten animals. About 30 subgroups hunt in the same area, near enough to hear one another. When a subgroup locates a school of anchovies, it quickly sends a message to the other subgroups, which rush to the area to help in the hunt.

After a hunt, the whole school stays together to socialize and then breaks into subgroups again to rest near shore, where there are fewer predators. During the winter months, when less food is available, the dolphins spend more time traveling in deep waters with their schools.

Nighttime hunters

New Zealand duskies spend the entire day in huge schools of hundreds of dolphins. They do not cooperate in herding fish as their South American cousins do. Their diet consists of fish and squid, which live in the deep ocean during the day. At night, these fish and squid move up closer to the ocean's surface, where the dolphins are able to grab them.

Atlantic spotted groups

Atlantic spotted dolphins are oceanic dolphins, but some live in inland waters, especially in summer. In the open ocean, schools can be as large as a hundred members. Dolphins that live near the coasts group themselves in small subgroups of five to twenty dolphins.

Atlantic spotted dolphins are very sociable and often swim within touching distance of one another. Two calves in the picture are nursing as they swim.

All together now!

Atlantic spotted subgroups consist of three to six dolphins that surface to breathe at the same time. Subgroup members travel in the same direction and stay within a few yards of one another. Some swim so close to one another that they never stop touching. Juvenile males tend to stay together in stable subgroups that do not change. Male adults also form stable subgroups. Young adults of both sexes sometimes swim with up to 50 individuals in a school. Nursery pods often swim together as subgroups.

The spotted dolphins above are surfacing together to breathe. They are a tightly knit group.

Mother-and-calf pairs are especially close. The calves swim under or alongside their mothers.

Bottlenose subgroups

Coastal bottlenose dolphins are smaller in size than their oceanic bottlenose cousins are, and so are their groups. Their herds are made up of as few as ten dolphins, and their subgroups have between two and four. Oceanic groups have up to 1,000 members.

Bottlenose subgroups

Different subgroups make up bottlenose herds. A mother-and-calf pair makes up a core group that stays together for up to six years, or until the mother has a new calf. Groups of mothers and calves often travel and hunt in a nursery pod. Juvenile males and females make up another subgroup whose members play together. The males in these groups form strong bonds. They compete for the most **dominant** positions in their groups through play. (See page 29.)

This bottlenose dolphin is fishing alone in a river. It turns upside down to see the fish better. Swimming upside down also prevents the dolphin from scraping its pectoral fins on the river bottom and makes it easier for the dolphin to swallow its prey. Sometimes two or more dolphins cooperate in driving fish onto a riverbank and beach themselves briefly to catch the fish.

Male alliances

Adult male bottlenose dolphins form **alliances** of two or three males that stay together for several years. Some bottlenose males form **superalliances** of up to fifteen males. They cooperate in hunting and herding females for the purpose of **mating**. Alliances have been known to attack other dolphins.

Orca family pods

Orcas live in cool ocean waters, especially near polar regions. There are two kinds of orca communities, but all orcas belong to one species. **Transient** orca pods live in deep ocean waters but also travel through areas where other orcas live. They travel alone or in small groups of about six animals. They eat mainly seals, porpoises, sea turtles, and some fish. They hunt quietly and cooperate in chasing their prey. To catch it, the orcas ram it with their heads, whack it with their tails, and **corral**, or surround it. **Resident** pods live near shorelines. They eat mainly fish and squid instead of marine mammals.

Transient orcas will chase marine mammals such as seals right up onto shore. They are fierce hunters.

Close family ties

Resident orcas form stable family groups called pods. The pods are made up of dolphins that are related to the same female **matriarchs**, or mothers. A **clan** is made up of a number of pods that share a similar vocal **dialect**, or set of sounds used to communicate. A **community** includes all the pods that regularly gather together.

Stable groups

Calves and mothers form lifelong bonds. Daughters, mothers, and grandmothers often stay together. Family pods offer calves opportunities to gain skills that will keep them safe and alive for years to come. With each generation, new orcas are added to the pods.

Subpods and superpods

When pods grow large, daughters with calves sometimes start their own subpods within the pod. In late summer or fall, **superpods**, or clusters of pods, gather to mate. They leap, slap the water with their flippers and flukes, and greet one another with strokes and belly rubs. Orcas also perform spectacular **breaches**, or full-body leaps, such as the one shown at the top of page 16.

Some orcas hunt marine mammals, but wild orcas do not pose a threat to humans.

Dolphin days

There is no such thing as a typical day in a dolphin's life. Different dolphins live in different ways. There are, however, things that all dolphins do. All dolphins swim, dive, rest, play, travel, mate, and avoid predators, but the most important activity in a dolphin's day is finding food. Many species of dolphins hunt in groups.

Swimming and diving

To find food and avoid predators, dolphins need to swim fast and dive deep. They can swim quickly because their streamlined shapes allow them to glide through water. They can dive deep and hold their breath for up to fifteen minutes because their bodies are able to use each breath efficiently. Dolphins use up to 90 percent of their lung capacity and can empty and refill their lungs in a fifth of a second. They are also able to store much more oxygen in their muscles and blood than land animals can.

Time for a nap!

Like other animals, dolphins need to rest. While most animals sleep, they breathe without thinking, but dolphins are **voluntary breathers**. They must make a conscious effort to breathe. Scientists think that dolphins rest one side of their brains at a time and breathe with the other side. If they fall into a deep sleep, they will drown. Dolpins take naps near the ocean's surface, where they can breathe easily.

Dolphins do not need much rest because water supports the weight of their bodies. They can take short naps and be ready to go again.

Some dolphins hunt at night, and others hunt during the day or at dawn and dusk. Some, such as these spinner dolphins, are part of big schools, and others spend their time in small groups. Some like people, and others do not go near them.

In touch with the pod

Dolphins need to be in touch with one another in order to hunt, mate, and fend off predators. Apart from these survival reasons, dolphins seem to enjoy the company of other dolphins! To communicate with one another, dolphins use sounds and body language.

Dolphin talk

Dolphins have no vocal cords and cannot move their mouths, lips, or tongues to form words. Dolphin "talk" includes sounds such as clicks, whistles, grunts, barks, and squeaks. Humans do not know for sure what the sounds mean, but dolphins understand the noises made by other dolphins and often change their behavior when they hear certain sounds.

"I am here!"

Scientists have learned that every dolphin has its own identifying sound. The sound is called a **signature whistle**, and it is used like a name. A dolphin announces its arrival by calling out its whistle name. It calls other dolphins by **mimicking**, or imitating, their signature whistles. When mothers and calves are part of a large group, they constantly whistle to one another to make sure they do not lose contact.

Members of large schools may know up to 500 dolphins. They touch one another often to establish the trust required for cooperative hunting.

Pod body language

Dolphins also communicate using gestures and movements. When a pod acts as a team, each dolphin must be able to understand what is about to happen. A signal such as a fin movement made by one pod member may tell other members that there is a predator nearby. The dolphins might then swim close together in a tight group to protect one another. Jumps may communicate the location of prey.

Showing emotion

Dolphins also use body language to show emotion. If a dolphin is angry, it may slap or thrash its tail, clap its jaws, or **gape**. To gape is to open the jaws wide. Most of the time, however, dolphins are very friendly with one another. They stroke each other with their pectoral fins, gently nip each other, and keep their group members in sight. Mothers are especially affectionate with their calves and touch them often. Dolphins have sensitive skin, and they seem to enjoy being touched!

(top) A small fin movement made by one dolphin can communicate important information to others.
(bottom) Groups of dolphins, such as this pantropical spotted dolphin group, sometimes gape to show aggression.

Mating and babies

*While swimming, a calf is carried along by an envelope of water flowing past its mother's body. Swimming in this position is called **echelon swimming**.*

The mating game

Dolphins become adults between the ages of five and sixteen years and can then make babies. Most females wait until they are much older, however. Females **reproduce**, or have babies, every one to eight years. Those with calves seldom mate until their calves stop nursing. The males compete to mate with the females. In some species, dolphins from many pods come together in the spring and fall to mate. Other species may breed throughout the year. Male dolphins have no role in raising the calves.

Staying with their moms

Depending on the species, dolphin babies **gestate**, or grow inside their mothers, for nine to fifteen months until they are ready to be born. Most are born tail first, but some **emerge** headfirst. Calves often stay with their mothers until they are ready to have their own babies. They learn the rules of pod behavior from their mothers and other pod members. Although dolphins give birth to one calf at a time, they can have many offspring because they live a long time—between 25 and 90 years—depending on the species!

Helping with the birth

When bottlenose calves are born, the females in a nursery pod surround the birthing mother to protect her and her calf from predators. Female dolphins of other species also help the birthing mothers of their pods, sometimes guiding the babies to the surface of the water for their first breath.

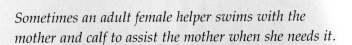

These dolphins form a ring of protection around a birthing mother and her newborn calf. They point their tails outward, ready to whack any predators that may swim by.

Sometimes an adult female helper swims with the mother and calf to assist the mother when she needs it.

Protecting the calf

A calf swims under or alongside its mother. In a school, mothers and babies are often surrounded by other dolphins for protection. Some nursery pods have adult helpers that care for the calves while the mothers hunt. As soon as the calf is old enough, it learns to hunt from its mother. The rest of a calf's time is taken up by playing. Adult dolphins protect the playing calves by keeping them in the center of a pod or school.

A mother dolphin squirts milk into her calf's mouth from her nipples, which are located inside two slits near her tail. The milk is rich in fat and protein, which help the baby grow quickly and add a thick layer of blubber to its body. Most calves nurse for about two years, but some nurse until they are adults.

Hunting in groups

Dolphins are not born with the **instinct**, or unlearned knowledge, of how to hunt. They learn how to hunt by watching other dolphins. They do not just learn old ways of hunting, however. They use their intelligence to invent a variety of hunting methods.

carousel method

Search, detect, and catch

Many dolphins use the **search-detect-catch** hunting method. Two or three scouts swim out to sea to locate prey, while other dolphins swim in the same direction as that of the scouts but closer to shore. When the scouts detect prey, all the dolphins rush out to sea to help "round up" the fish.

Chasing prey

Some orcas and false killer whales use their excellent senses of sight and hearing to catch prey. They hunt quietly because any sound could alert the animals. Transient orcas often whack their prey with their flukes or toss it into the air and play with it. Resident orca pods might fan out over a large area to look for salmon. When they have found food, they may leap out of the water to let others know where it is. They then use the **carousel method**, shown above, to trap their prey. They circle the fish and drive them into a tight ball. Many other species of dolphins also use this method of hunting.

A fine kettle of fish!

*The **kettle method** is similar to the carousel method. Dolphins swim quickly above and below a school of fish, creating a whirlpool effect, such as when water is stirred in a kettle, or pot. Once the fish are spun into a tight bunch, the dolphins dive in and grab their meal. Dolphins feed in the same way when using the carousel method.*

Other ways of trapping fish

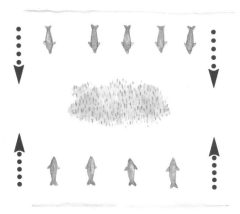

The dolphins cooperate in trapping fish between two walls of dolphins.

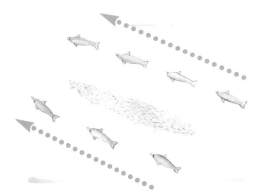

(above) Dolphins work together to herd prey. They herd it into places where it is easier to catch, as shown in the following diagrams.

These dolphins are herding fish into a tight ball against the surface of the ocean, where the fish cannot escape.

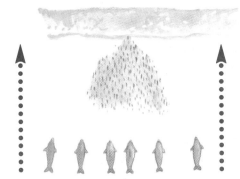

These fish are being driven against shore, where there is also no escape.

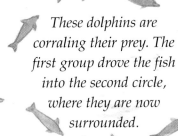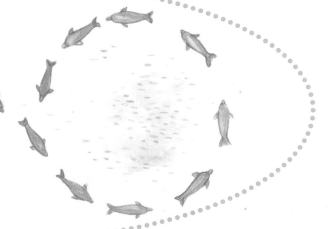

These dolphins are corraling their prey. The first group drove the fish into the second circle, where they are now surrounded.

25

Hunting with echolocation

These Atlantic spotted dolphins are using echolocation in groups. The group on the left has found some fish hiding in the sand.

When they cannot use their vision, dolphins use **sonar**, or **echolocation**, to find food. Echolocation means producing sounds and using their echoes to locate something. Dolphins use this method of "seeing and hearing" alone and in groups. They know when to use or not use this special sense. If prey is easy to see, dolphins do not use echolocation because the sounds it produces might warn the prey. When there is no prey in sight, dolphin schools often fan out and use echolocation to scan the ocean for food.

Sending and receiving

Dolphins have fatty deposits in their melons and lower jaws. This special fat allows them to send and receive sounds. A dolphin creates clicking sounds in the nasal passages below its blowhole and directs the sounds with its melon. The sounds bounce back as echoes to the dolphin's jaw and travel to its ear and then to its brain. A large part of a dolphin's brain is used to interpret the information received from the echoes, which paint an accurate "sound picture" in the brain.

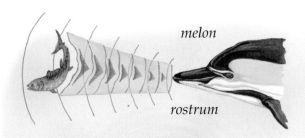

melon

rostrum

How echolocation works

To use echolocation, a dolphin creates clicking sounds. It then uses its melon (see page 6) to focus the sound beam. The sound strikes an object and returns to the dolphin's jaw as an echo. The dolphin continues to send and receive clicks. It can measure the distance of the object by the length of time that passes between the echoes. Echoes also give details about the object's size, shape, and nature.

Using echolocation, this bottlenose dolphin has found a fish hidden in the sand and is now digging it up.

A dolphin can send out as many as 700 clicks per second to determine the size, location, and nature of an object. This Atlantic spotted dolphin is enjoying a fish it located with its sonar.

Time to play!

Dolphins love to play, and playing is an important way for them to get to know one another. Dolphins that are a part of large schools socialize with several hundred school members through play. While they feed, they often toss their food high in the air several times before they swallow it. Tossing food may just be a game of "catch" or a method of teaching calves the art of hunting. Tossing food may also be a way for dolphins to learn to trust one another. A dolphin needs to know that no other dolphin will steal its food.

These Atlantic spotted dolphins are playing a game with a bandanna that they have found. The one carrying it will let it go, and another will catch it with a fin, fluke, or in its mouth. Catch is a favorite game among wild dolphins.

Jumping for joy!

Dolphins dance, splash, and perform spectacular spins, rollovers, tail walks, and head-over-tail jumps. Sometimes two or three dolphins leap at the same time. Many dolphins like to **bow-ride**, or get pushed along by the waves in front of boats. They also enjoy **wake-riding** behind boats, where they can surf the waves the boats create.

*These dolphins are demonstrating the game described in the artwork below. Instead of turning to one side, one is leaping over the other in a **crossover jump**, which looks a lot like a game of leapfrog.*

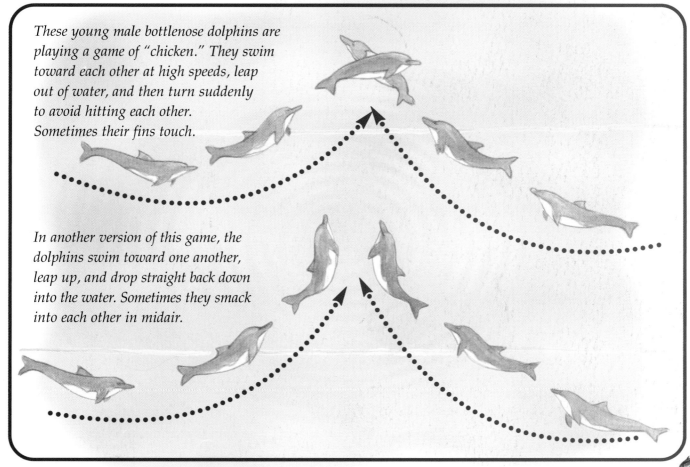

These young male bottlenose dolphins are playing a game of "chicken." They swim toward each other at high speeds, leap out of water, and then turn suddenly to avoid hitting each other. Sometimes their fins touch.

In another version of this game, the dolphins swim toward one another, leap up, and drop straight back down into the water. Sometimes they smack into each other in midair.

Pod mysteries

It is difficult to study dolphin pods in the wild because dolphins are constantly on the move and spend most of their time underwater. Scientists study wild dolphins by observing their surface behavior from boats and airplanes, by tracking them with small radio transmitters attached to their dorsal fins, and by swimming with them. Although people have studied dolphins for many years, pod behavior is still largely a mystery to humans.

Nursing grannies

Pilot whales are very social and affectionate with one another. Their pods not only include mothers and their offspring but also grand-mothers that are still nursing their last calves,

which are adults! Scientists do not know why these grannies continue to nurse, but they think this behavior may have to do with how pilot whales find food. Pilot whales hunt squid at depths of about 2,000 feet (600 m). When the pod is diving for food, the grannies may look after the calves that cannot dive deep and feed them milk while their mothers hunt.

On the beach

Pilot whales are part of another pod mystery—**strandings**. No one knows why a dolphin strands, or beaches itself. A single stranding may be caused by **parasites** in a dolphin's inner ear. Parasites may make a dolphin lose its sense of direction and swim onto a beach.

Mass strandings

Mass strandings, which involve whole herds of dolphins, are more mysterious. They may be the result of loud sounds, such as navy **LFAS**, which is believed to cause severe ear and brain damage in ocean creatures.

Mass strandings may also result from a change in the earth's **magnetic field**, causing deep-ocean dolphins, such as the long-finned pilot whales, shown above, to lose their sense of direction. A dolphin's sonar also may not work properly during storms.

Tuna-net mysteries

For unknown reasons, large schools of tuna gather under dolphin pods, so when fishers catch the fish, they also trap dolphins. **Purse-seine nets**, show right, are designed to allow dolphins to escape. Although some trapped dolphins simply wait to be released from the net, others are too frightened to leave even when the net is lowered. In some cases, the dolphins will not swim out unless there is a large enough opening for most of their pod members to leave. Some scientists think that the dolphins may not leave because they sense that they will not be able to survive without a certain number of pod members.

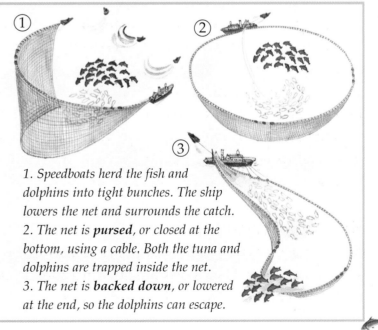

1. Speedboats herd the fish and dolphins into tight bunches. The ship lowers the net and surrounds the catch.
2. The net is **pursed**, or closed at the bottom, using a cable. Both the tuna and dolphins are trapped inside the net.
3. The net is **backed down**, or lowered at the end, so the dolphins can escape.

Glossary

Note: Words that are defined in the book may not appear in the glossary.

alliance An association of two or more dolphins that cooperate for a purpose such as hunting

camouflage Colors and patterns used by animals to blend in with their environment in order to hide

dominant Describing an animal that controls or commands others

emerge To come out or appear

fission-fusion Describing dolphin groups that split into smaller groups and then join up again

instinct A pattern of behavior that is not learned but with which an animal is born

juvenile Describing an animal that is not yet mature

LFAS Low Frequency Active Sonar; very loud and dangerous sound waves, produced by navy sonar equipment, that hurt or kill ocean creatures

magnetic field The electric current that pulls towards the poles of the earth

mating The act of joining together to make babies

parasite An organism that lives off another

predator An animal that hunts and eats other animals in order to survive

prey An animal that is hunted by a predator

reproduce To produce offspring

resident Living in one place or area

species Living things that closely resemble one another and are able to breed together

strand To come ashore and become helpless to return to water

transient Describing an animal that stays in one place for only a short time

warm-blooded Describing an animal whose body temperature stays about the same and does not change with its surroundings

Index

1 2 3 4 5 6 7 8 9 0   Printed in the U.S.A.   2 1 0 9 8 7 6 5 4 3